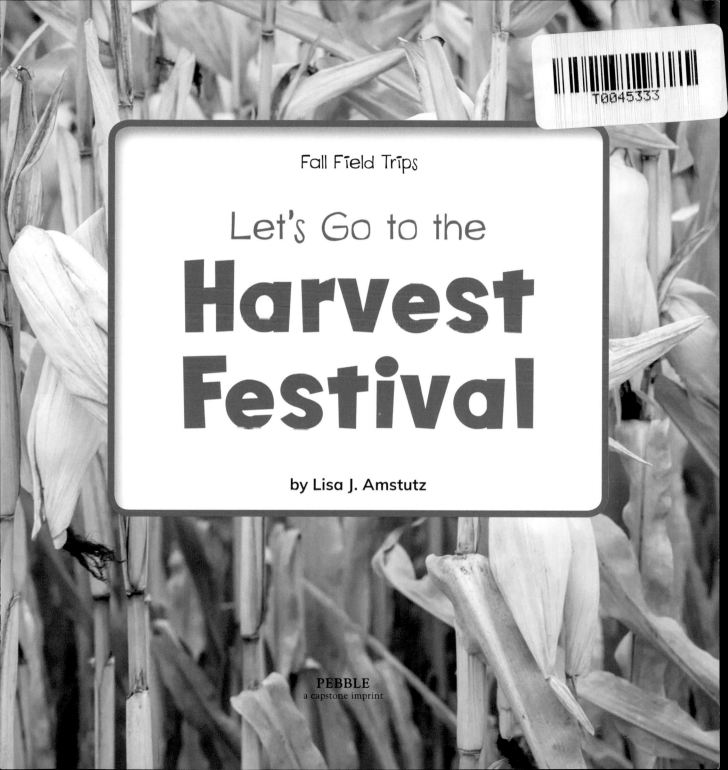

Fall Field Trips

# Let's Go to the
# Harvest Festival

by Lisa J. Amstutz

PEBBLE
a capstone imprint

Pebble Emerge is published by Pebble, an imprint of Capstone.
1710 Roe Crest Drive
North Mankato, Minnesota 56003
www.capstonepub.com

**Library of Congress Cataloging-in-Publication Data is available on the Library
of Congress website.**
ISBN 978-1-9771-2448-7 (library binding)
ISBN 978-1-9771-2491-3 (eBook PDF)

Summary: It's fall, and it's time to go to a harvest festival! Learn about harvests,
see the food and treats, and have some fun celebrating too. Through playful text
and beautiful images, kids will experience what it's like to go to a harvest festival.

**Image Credits**
iStockphoto: Juanmonino, Cover; Newscom: Leila Navidi/ZUMA Press, 13, Richard
Sennott/ZUMA Press, 12; Shutterstock: Adam Frank, 17, AllNikArt, (pumpkin)
design element throughout, AShi Yali, 19, bbernard, 5, Helen's Photos, 9, Kim
Wilder Hinson, 6, Mostovyi Sergii Igorevich, 20, Nella, 3, NeydtStock, 11, solarus,
(plaid) design element, Suzanne Tucker, 7, Vicki L. Miller, 15, VIIIPhotography, 1

**Editorial Credits**
Editor: Shelly Lyons; Designer: Kayla Rossow; Media Researcher: Morgan Walters;
Production Specialist: Spencer Rosio

All internet sites appearing in back matter were available and accurate when this
book was sent to press.

Printed and bound in China
PO3322

# Table of Contents

Words in **bold** are in the glossary.

# A Trip to the Harvest Festival

The air feels cool! It's time to wear coats. We wear hats and gloves too. Leaves turn orange and gold. Can you guess what **season** it is? It is fall!

In fall, farmers pick **crops**. They **harvest** vegetables such as corn and beans. Fruits such as apples and pumpkins are picked too. It is time to visit a harvest **festival**!

# A Taste of Fall

At the festival, good smells fill the air. There are lots of things to eat here. Popcorn pops in a big **kettle**. Meat sizzles on a hot grill.

We fill our plates with good food. Green
beans are steamed and ready to eat.
We butter warm corn on the cob. Then
we take a bite. *Crunch!*

Are you ready for dessert? Let's try an apple fritter. The fried treat smells like warm apples. The powdered sugar sticks to our hands.

Now let's taste the pumpkin pie. We add a scoop of whipped cream. The pie is smooth and creamy in our mouths. Mmm! It tastes like spices and sweet pumpkin.

# So Much to Do!

It's time to make a silly scarecrow! A scarecrow keeps birds from feeding on crops. We stuff a shirt and pants with straw. A pumpkin makes a good head.

We add eyes and a mouth. A pine cone makes a good nose. A black hat sits on the head. Stay away birds!

A corn pit is filled with hard yellow kernels. It is fun to play in. We hide our feet in the corn. We scoop and dig.

Next we try the giant slide. We climb steps to the top. One, two, three! We push off and slide. It's a quick ride down to the ground. Whee!

A whistle blows. All aboard! Here comes a tiny train. It is made of old barrels. We climb on for a ride. A tractor pulls the train. We wave at people walking by.

15

# Time to Dance

It's time to dance! Someone plays a musical **instrument** called a fiddle. She pulls a bow across the strings. The strings make music. We dance and spin.

Now everyone is tired. We roast marshmallows over a fire. Chocolate and crackers are added to make s'mores. They are sticky but tasty treats.

People all around the world **celebrate** the harvest. They welcome fall. They give thanks for good crops. People eat and play and dance. Did you have fun at the harvest festival? Let's go again next year!

19

# Make a Leaf Print

Frame your leaf prints or cut them out and string them together to make a chain.

## What You Need:

- leaves of different shapes and sizes (soft ones work better)

- paper (2 sheets)
- paint
- paintbrush
- rolling pin

## What You Do:

1. Coat one side of a leaf with a thin layer of paint.

2. Place the painted side down on a sheet of paper.

3. Lay the second sheet of paper on top.

4. Gently roll over both sheets with the rolling pin.

5. Carefully remove the top sheet and the leaf. Let the paint dry.

# Glossary

**celebrate** (SE-luh-brayt)—to do something fun on a special day

**crop** (KROP)—a plant farmers grow in large amounts, usually for food; farmers grow crops such as corn, soybeans, and peas

**festival** (FES-tuh-vuhl)—a holiday or party

**harvest** (HAR-vist)—to gather crops that are ready to be picked

**instrument** (IN-struh-muhnt)—something used to make music

**kettle** (KET-uhl)—a large metal cooking pot, usually with a handle

**season** (SEE-zuhn)—one of the four parts of the year; winter, spring, summer, and fall are seasons

# Read More

Rustad, Martha E. H. *Fall Harvest Fun.* Minneapolis: Lerner Publications, 2019.

Shores, Erika L. *Harvest Time.* North Mankato, MN: Capstone Press, 2016.

# Internet Sites

*17 Fun Harvest Festival Crafts*
*http://www.eparenting.co.uk/activities_for_kids/harvest_festival_activities_for_kids.php*

*Junior Master Gardener: Harvest Indicators*
*http://jmgkids.us/lgeg/grow/harvest-indicators/*

# Index